Learning About Loggerheads

My Observation Log
by Denise Bernard

Michelle Hyde Parsons
Illustrated by Daniel Del Valle

Harcourt Achieve

Rigby • Saxon • Steck-Vaughn

www.HarcourtAchieve.com
1.800.531.5015

April 25

In science class, we are learning about loggerhead turtles. Loggerhead turtles are a type of sea turtle. Every spring and summer, loggerheads lay their eggs on beaches here in Florida. Our teacher, Mrs. Payo, gave us a project to observe, or watch, loggerhead turtles for the next 15 weeks. We will all keep an observation log and write down what we see. Our school is open all year, so we will be working on our project during the summer.

Loggerhead Turtle Facts	
Length	up to 3 feet
Weight	up to 350 pounds
Where they live	on the coast of the Atlantic Ocean
What they eat	crabs, clams, jellyfish, and some plants

April 27

Today was the first day of our fifteen-week project, so we walked to the beach with Mrs. Payo. At the beach, we met Dr. Ortiz, a scientist who studies loggerhead turtles. He explained that loggerhead turtles **migrate** thousands of miles from the ocean back to the same beach where they hatched. Then they build nests and lay eggs. I wonder how the turtles know where to go!

school

beach

N
NW NE
W E
SW SE
S

Dr. Ortiz works with a team of scientists, and they took us on a boat to look for loggerheads. While we were on the boat, Dr. Ortiz looked at his computer and told us that there was a loggerhead turtle swimming nearby. Dr. Ortiz drove the boat to where the turtle was swimming. He said that he recognized the turtle and that her name was Lucy.

This is Dr. Ortiz and me.

Dr. Ortiz's team gently pulled Lucy onto the boat to weigh and measure her. Lucy was 4 feet long and weighed 300 pounds! Her huge head was covered with **barnacles,** which are tiny animals that look like shells. I couldn't believe how big Lucy was. Lucy waved her flippers and tried to get away. Some of my classmates were scared of her, but I thought she was beautiful.

barnacles

flipper

This is a picture of Lucy.

May 6

This afternoon we went to the library, and I learned some more facts about loggerheads. I read that they are called loggerheads because their heads are so large. I also read that there are only about 200,000 loggerheads in the world. In some parts of the United States, more and more loggerheads are dying every year.

There are many reasons why loggerhead turtles are dying. Pollution in the ocean can kill the turtles. Animals sometimes eat the baby turtles. Also, many turtles die when they get caught in fishing nets. If we do not **protect** them, loggerheads might become **extinct.** This means that one day there might not be any loggerheads alive at all.

Today in science class we learned that loggerheads build their nests and lay eggs only at night. I'm so happy because tonight we will make a special trip to the beach. Our parents will come with us.

We haven't visited the beach in a long time, so I hope we will see a turtle lay its eggs tonight.

This is what I will wear to the beach tonight.

May 28

Last night was excellent! We went to the beach and met Dr. Ortiz and his team. It was chilly and really quiet except for the sound of the waves hitting the beach. And it was so dark that I couldn't see my watch! We all saw a large turtle coming out of the water, and it had barnacles on its head. It was Lucy!

As Lucy moved along the beach, she left a trail behind her that looked like giant tire tracks in the sand. We hid so we wouldn't bother her. (Mrs. Payo said that if turtles are scared before they build their nests, they won't lay their eggs.) We waited for Lucy to find the best place for her nest.

Lucy crawled across the beach until she got to a place where the waves couldn't reach her. Mrs. Payo said that loggerheads build their nests in this place so the water won't wash away the eggs.

It took Lucy about an hour to dig her nest. First she used her front flippers to dig a pit about the same size as her body. Then she used her back flippers to dig a deep hole.

We watched as Lucy laid her eggs. It took her about 20 minutes to lay all of her eggs. The eggs were soft, and they looked like golf balls. Some of them bounced as they landed in the nest!

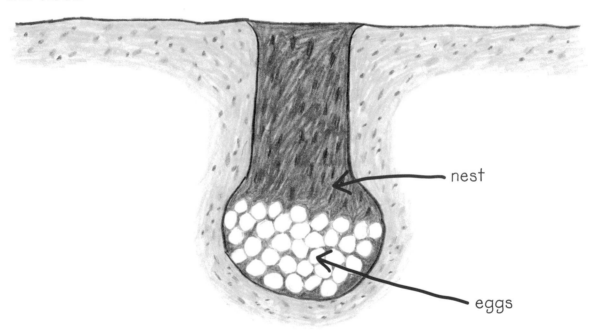

nest

eggs

Here is a picture of a loggerhead nest.

I thought Lucy was crying because I saw tears flowing down her face. Dr. Ortiz explained that loggerhead turtles look like they're crying when they lay their eggs. He said that turtles drink saltwater from the ocean, and the tears wash away the salt that is in the turtles' bodies. The tears also wash the sand out of the turtles' eyes.

After Lucy had laid all of her eggs, she covered them. Gently, she pushed sand into the hole and patted it down. Then she threw sand around with her front flippers. Dr. Ortiz said that she was throwing the sand around because she was hiding her nest.

When Lucy was finished, Dr. Ortiz put a bright orange sign next to the nest so people would not disturb, or bother it.

Lucy was out of the water for about two hours. I think she was very tired because on her way back to the ocean, she stopped to rest a lot. When she finally reached the shore, the waves lifted her into the water, and then she was gone. I was sad because I didn't know if I would ever see Lucy again.

Mrs. Payo said it would take about two months for the eggs to hatch. It will be so hard to wait that long!

May 29

In science class today we studied the **life cycle** of loggerhead turtles. A loggerhead turtle can live for up to 50 years. When a female loggerhead is between 20 and 30 years old, she will build a nest and lay her eggs on a beach. (The male loggerheads spend their entire lives in the ocean and never go back on land.) Two months later, the baby turtles, called **hatchlings,** come out of the nest. The hatchlings spend many years out in the ocean and become adults. When the female turtles are ready to lay their eggs, they return to the same beach where they hatched as babies.

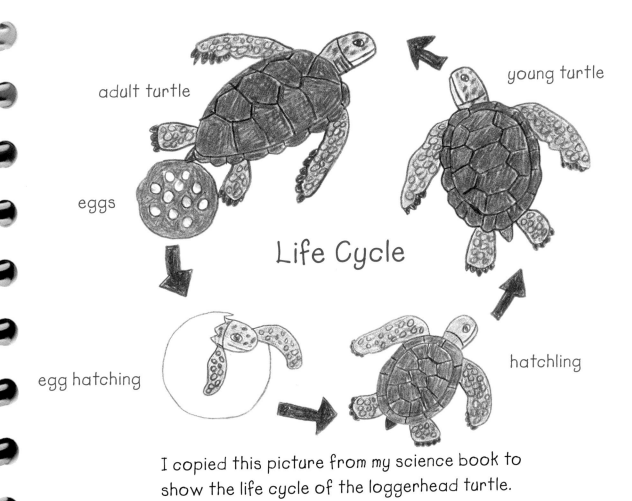

adult turtle

young turtle

eggs

Life Cycle

egg hatching

hatchling

I copied this picture from my science book to show the life cycle of the loggerhead turtle.

July 8

It has been seven weeks since Lucy laid her eggs. Raccoons, crabs, and sea birds all like to eat turtle eggs, so we have been checking the nest often to make sure it is okay. Each week we would take turns visiting the beach at night with our parents. We have also been visiting the library to learn more about loggerhead turtles.

I learned that the hatchlings have a special egg-tooth that helps them break through the eggshell. It takes the hatchlings several days to dig out of the nest. When they dig, they move their flippers as if they are swimming up through the sand.

Only one out of 1,000 sea turtles lives long enough to lay eggs.

July 9

We visited the beach again this afternoon, and I noticed a small dent in the top of Lucy's nest. I was worried, but Dr. Ortiz said the dent was there because the eggs were going to hatch soon. We watched the nest for a while, but nothing happened. We didn't see any hatchlings today, but I know that we only have to wait a little longer.

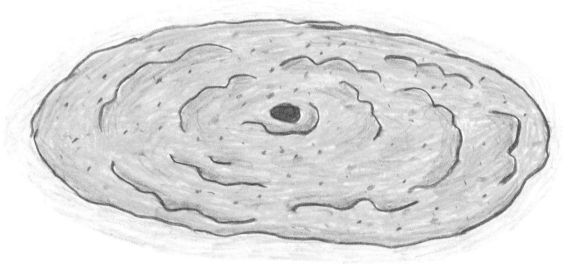

We finally saw the hatchlings! Mrs. Payo explained that hatchlings usually come out of the nest at night. So last night we made a special trip to the beach. First we heard sounds coming from the nest. Then the dent in the nest got bigger, and a hole appeared. I saw a tiny claw, and a little hatchling dug itself out of the sand. It was smaller than an orange!

The hatchlings were so cute as they crawled out of the nest. Then they crawled toward the ocean. I learned that during their journey to the ocean, many things can hurt the hatchlings. Sunlight can kill them if they take too long to reach the water. **Predators,** or animals that eat other animals, can also eat the hatchlings.

We watched the hatchlings until they reached the ocean and floated away. I said goodbye and wished them a safe journey.

Today was the last day of our project, so we went to the beach again. Dr. Ortiz said that Lucy's hatchlings would spend about a year floating in the ocean. Then their shells would become hard, and predators would leave them alone. I can't believe that it will be 30 years before they return to lay their eggs!

We said goodbye to Dr. Ortiz and thanked him for helping us learn so much about loggerheads. It was a great adventure!

Glossary

barnacles tiny sea animals that attach themselves to rocks and other sea animals

extinct no longer existing

hatchling a sea turtle that has recently hatched

life cycle the stages of an animal's life

migrate to move from one area to another

predator an animal that hunts another animal for food

protect to keep safe from harm

Index